CODE NAME: THE LONG SOBBING

Right: *Verräter* (traitor), poster by Max Spielmanns, warns the public against listening to foreign broadcasts which was deemed an act of treason. Germany, 1944.

"This is London calling, the European News Service of the British Broadcasting Corporation. Here is the news, but first here are some messages for our friends in occupied countries: the Trojan War will not be held, John is growing a very long beard this week, the long sobs of the violins of autumn, les sanglots longs des violons de l'automne…"
— *Pierre Holmes, BBC Announcer*

Above: The broadcast of the first part of a verse of Paul Verlaine's poem, *Chanson d'Automne,* was the signal to the French Resistance that the invasion was imminent. The second part was transmitted by the BBC at 10:15 P.M. on June 5, 1944, indicating that the invasion was scheduled to begin within the next 48 hours.

Les sanglots longs
Des violons
De l'automne
Blessent mon coeur
D'une langueur
Monotone.

PAUL VERLAINE

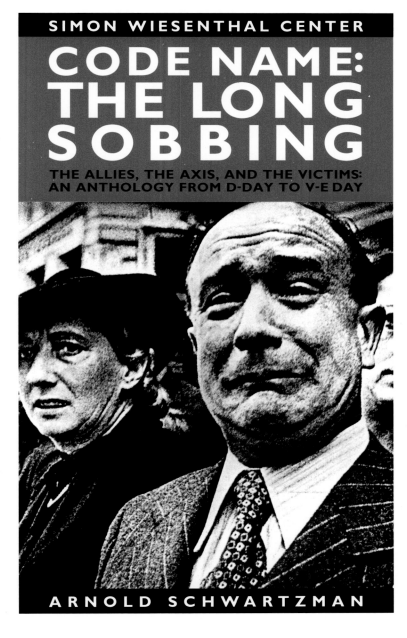

SIMON WIESENTHAL CENTER

CODE NAME: THE LONG SOBBING

THE ALLIES, THE AXIS, AND THE VICTIMS: AN ANTHOLOGY FROM D-DAY TO V-E DAY

ARNOLD SCHWARTZMAN

The long sobs
Of the violins
Of autumn,
Wounds my heart
With a monotonous
Languor.

CONTENTS

Design: Arnold Schwartzman
Editing and Production: Isolde Schwartzman

ISBN 0-943058-18-X

Printed in Hong Kong through Palace Press International
San Francisco

10 9 8 7 6 5 4 3 2 1

Simon Wiesenthal Center
9760 West Pico Boulevard
Los Angeles, CA 90035, U.S.A.

Title page: A tearful French
citizen watches as Nazis
occupy his homeland, 1940.
UPI / MOVIETONE NEWS

IT'S LONG AGO AND FAR AWAY, but I clearly recall the vision of my mother as she emerged with tears in her eyes from the aisles of the Odeon Cinema. I had been waiting outside in the vestibule while she watched the H-rated (British film censor classification for horror) film of the liberation of the Nazi concentration camps. Her sobs anticipated the fate of members of our family in Europe, who had perished in the Holocaust. Miraculously, my cousins who had served in the British Armed Forces at Dunkirk, D-Day, and Arnhem, as well as one who was incarcerated in a Japanese prisoner of war camp on Formosa, and another, whose ship was sunk by a torpedo, all returned safely.

The newsreels, which I had been excluded from viewing as a child, have now become familiar to me—scenes of General Eisenhower inspecting a concentration camp, and the liberation of the many other camps, have become the raw material of my craft.

The General, as the Supreme Allied Commander, had masterminded "Operation Overlord," the D-Day landings, which ultimately brought about the liberation of Europe.

Almost a year after the largest armada in history had been assembled in "Piccadilly Circus", the rendezvous point in the English Channel, my parents and I stood among the jubilant assembly in Piccadilly Circus, London, to celebrate V-E Day.

I was four years old when the London Blitz began, living in the city's Jewish Quarter, the East End. Located in close proximity to the London docks, an important supply line for the country, this area was an obvious target for Hitler's Luftwaffe—thus the Führer was able to "kill two birds with one stone"! Indeed, Hitler was fighting two wars, one against the Allies, and another against the Jews. Hermann Göring said of the London Blitz: "This will strike a blow right into the enemy's heart."

My recollections are limited, but vivid, of that first day of aerial bombing: September 7, 1940 was a hot afternoon, and the Sabbath before the Jewish New Year, when the air raid warning sounded. My mother had just placed three salads on the dining room table—this was to be my last image of our home before it suffered a direct hit by an incendiary bomb. After being pulled out of the rubble by rescue workers, we spent the next few nights moving from street shelter to Tube station, from warehouse to schoolroom—eventually we were put on a bus and evacuated to the relative safety of the

Right: A Heinkel III, one of 400 German planes flying over the River Thames on the afternoon of September 7, 1940, was taken moments before Schwartzman's home, one mile to the north, suffered a direct hit and was destroyed by an incendiary bomb.
IMPERIAL WAR MUSEUM   C5422

8th June, 1946

TO-DAY, AS WE CELEBRATE VICTORY, I send this personal message to you and all other boys and girls at school. For you have shared in the hardships and dangers of a total war and you have shared no less in the triumph of the Allied Nations.

I know you will always feel proud to belong to a country which was capable of such supreme effort; proud, too, of parents and elder brothers and sisters who by their courage, endurance and enterprise brought victory. May these qualities be yours as you grow up and join in the common effort to establish among the nations of the world unity and peace.

George R.I.

Above: King George VI's message distributed to all schoolchildren in Great Britain at the end of World War II.

countryside. To this day, the wail of an air raid siren never fails to send a Pavlovian shudder down my spine.

Turbaned and in a boiler suit, my mother worked in a munitions factory—I believed for the sole purpose that she construct for me model Spitfires; while my father worked as a headwaiter at The Savoy, where he would serve Prime Minister Winston Churchill, a frequent patron, his favorite dish of chicken soup—and at night my father served as a fire-watcher on the hotel's roof.

Often, American servicemen who dined at the hotel would give my father their copies of *Life* and *Saturday Evening Post* magazines, and I fantasized about the American way of life as depicted in Norman Rockwell's covers.

I also escaped into the world of *Dumbo*, and *Bambi*, Abbott and Costello, and Laurel and Hardy. The reality was a world of ration books, powdered milk and dried eggs, blackout curtains and gas masks, cigarette cards and barrage balloons, and pockets full of shrapnel collected from the ever burgeoning number of bomb sites.

The password between British schoolchildren and the friendly invaders, the "Yanks," was: "Got any gum, chum?" while the grown-ups jealously described them as "overpaid, oversexed, and over here."

Browsing through my collection of ephemera, I came across copies of two of the most popular British war-time magazines, *Picture Post* and *Lilliput*. It struck me that the latter's concept of juxtaposing two related images side by side had subconsciously guided my visual philosophy in film and design. I have carried this notion throughout this book with visual connections such as the image of the battalion of soldiers I once saw exercising on the beaches of Blackpool in preparation for D-Day, standing with their arms outstretched, and the similar image of row upon row of crosses I recently photographed in a military cemetery in Normandy.

Standing on the deck of the R.M.S. Queen Mary—another ex-patriot, now docked a few miles from my home in Southern California—I thought back to my "salad days," when this ship ferried many thousands of U.S. troops to England in preparation for the D-Day invasion; and where the planned amphibious assault was first demonstrated by the military commanders to Winston Churchill by floating model ships in his cabin's bathtub! This was also the ship that after the war took my cousin as a G.I. bride to these shores, and where my uncle, one of the ship's bandleaders, would lead his orchestra in playing the 1940s Jerome Kern hit: *Long Ago And Far Away*.

In producing this "scrapbook" on World War II, the images became my aide-mémoire to the making of the film *Code Name: The Long Sobbing*. I hope this book will serve as a useful companion to the documentary film, which chronicles the events from D-Day, June 6, 1944, to V-E Day, May 8, 1945, while also focusing on Hitler's unrelenting war against the Jews.

ARNOLD SCHWARTZMAN
Hollywood, 1994

Below: During her years of war service, the R.M.S. Queen Mary carried over 800,000 servicemen.

Above: Schwartzman, aged 9, dressed for the V-E Day street party. The blackout curtains now drawn, his father decorated the windows with a V···— for Victory, Union Jacks, and a photograph of Winston Churchill. Egham, Surrey. Great Britain, 1945.

Above: Corporal Adolf Hitler
with his comrades during WWI.
BUNDESARCHIV

Right: The candidate.
March 1932.
THE ILLUSTRATED LONDON NEWS

Opposite: *In the Beginning Was
the Word*. In this painting by
H. O. Hoyer, Adolf Hitler
mesmerizes his audience prior
to his election as Chancellor
of the German Republic. The
painting was widely reproduced
during the Third Reich.

HERR ADOLF HITLER, THE NATIONAL
SOCIALIST CANDIDATE IN THE GERMAN
PRESIDENTIAL ELECTION.

Above: Special "charity" issue postage stamp featuring the "Führer". Germany, 1936.

Right: *Der Sieg des Glaubens* (The victory of faith), SA (Sturmabteilung: storm troopers) woodcut by Prof. R. Schwarzkopf. Germany, 1937.

Der Sieg des Glaubens.

Opposite: Reichschancellor Hitler and senior members of the SA.
BUNDESARCHIV

Right: Anti-semitic children's board game, *Juden raus!* (Jews out!). The game features a number of Jewish shops within the ancient walls of Jerusalem. Rules state: "Show skill with the dice, so that you can collect many Jews," and "If you can kick out 6 Jews, you are the winner without question." Germany, 1930s.
WIENER LIBRARY

Below: By a decree issued on October 5, 1938, German Jews had the letter J for Jude (Jew) stamped in their passports.
SIMON WIESENTHAL CENTER

Right: Sign on a Jewish shop: "I am Jewish. Aryans enter my shop at their own peril".

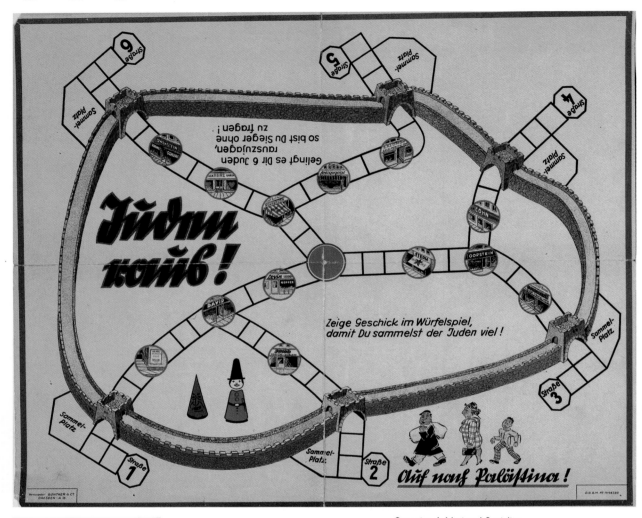

∴ Ich bin Jude ∴

Arier
betreten mein Geschäft
auf eigene Gefahr!

Opposite: A National Socialist Party boycott poster outside a Jewish shop, urging the German people not to buy from Jews. Berlin, 1930s.
BUNDESARCHIV

Above and opposite: Storm troopers picket Jewish establishments with placards proclaiming: "Germans! Defend yourselves! Do not buy from Jews!" Berlin, Germany, 1933.

BUNDESARCHIV

ÉTAT FRANÇAIS
DÉPARTEMENT DE SEINE-&-OISE
Avis aux Gestionnaires
d'Entreprises JUIVES

Une affiche en date du 18 Octobre 1940 a défini le caractère « d'entreprise juive », conformément aux instructions de l'Ordonnance du 18 Octobre des autorités allemandes.

Sont considérées comme juives aux termes de cette ordonnance les entreprises dont les propriétaires ou titulaires de bail :

1° Sont juifs ou

2° Société en nom collectif dont un associé est juif ou

3° Sociétés à responsabilité limitée dont plus d'un tiers des associés sont juifs ou dont plus d'un tiers des participations sont entre les mains d'associés juifs ou dont le gérant est juif ou dont plus d'un tiers des membres du conseil de surveillance sont juifs.

4° Sociétés anonymes dont le président du conseil d'administration ou un administrateur délégué ou plus d'un tiers des membres du conseil d'administration sont juifs.

Les propriétaires ou responsables de la gestion de ces entreprises sont invités à se présenter dans un délai maximum de 48 heures :
1° à la Chambre de Commerce dont ils dépendent,
soit à la Chambre de Commerce de Versailles, 6, rue Magenta ;
ou à la Chambre de Commerce de Corbeil, Hôtel de Ville.
2° S'ils sont artisans,
à la Chambre des Métiers, 14, rue Hoche, à Versailles ;
afin de régler une question importante concernant la gestion de leurs entreprises dans le cadre des instructions des autorités d'occupation.
Toute contravention à la présente affiche entraînera la fermeture de l'établissement.

Versailles, le 1er Décembre 1940.

Le Préfet de Seine-et-Oise
Marc CHEVALIER.

ÉTAT FRANÇAIS
VILLE DE MARSEILLE
ARRÊTÉ
relatif au
RECENSEMENT DES JUIFS

NOUS, Préfet des Bouches-du-Rhône, Administrateur Extraordinaire de la Ville de Marseille, Officier de la Légion d'Honneur ;
VU la loi du 3 Avril 1884 ;
VU le décret du 20 Mars 1939, pris en exécution du décret-loi du 12 Novembre 1939 ;
VU la loi du 29 Juillet 1940 ;
VU la loi du 2 Juin 1941 ;
VU la loi du 13 Juillet 1941 ;
VU l'article 471, paragraphe 15 du Code Pénal.

ARRÊTONS :

ARTICLE PREMIER. — Toute personne juive au regard de la loi du 2 Juin 1941 portant statut des juifs doit en faire la déclaration, sur un imprimé spécial, en l'Hôtel de Ville, service de la Police Administrative, avant le 31 Juillet 1941, délai de rigueur.

ART. 2. — La déclaration ne sera réputée accomplie que lorsque l'imprimé réglementaire aura été dûment rempli par les intéressés, et déposé, ou adressé par la poste en recommandé à l'Hôtel de Ville. Toute déclaration effectuée avant la publication du présent arrêté ou non souscrite au moyen de l'imprimé réglementaire est nulle et de nul effet.

ART. 3. — M. le Commissaire Central de Police, M. le Commandant de Gendarmerie, M. le Directeur de la Police Administrative sont chargés, chacun en ce qui le concerne, de veiller à l'exécution du présent arrêté.

Fait à Marseille, le 22 Juillet 1941.

P. le Préfet des Bouches-du-Rhône,
Administrateur Extraordinaire de la Ville de Marseille,
Le Secrétaire Général de la Préfecture délégué
PIERRE BARRAUD.

Imp. Municipal

Above and left: Three French Vichy Government proclamations:

1: Decree defining what was considered a Jewish enterprise. December 1, 1940.

2: Notice to Jews to report to the Authorities by July 31, 1941.

3: Final notice to Jews from the Occupying Authorities to report by October 2, 1940, and obtain an identity card.

VILLE DE CHAMPIGNY-SUR-MARNE
AVIS AUX ISRAÉLITES

A la demande des Autorités d'occupation, les Israélites devront se présenter, munis de pièces d'identité, à la Mairie de Champigny (Bureau du Recensement), avant le **2 OCTOBRE, dernier délai,** pour y remplir une fiche d'identité.

Faute de se présenter dans les délais prescrits, les personnes sus-visées s'exposeront aux mesures les plus sévères.

Champigny-sur-Marne, le 26 Septembre 1940.

LE MAIRE :
Gaston CHARDIN

Imp. Ch. THOMAS, 4, rue de Mulhouse (Gde-Rue, entre la Mairie et le Pont de Mulhouse) Nogent - Tronch. 04-70

Above: An anti-semitic sign displayed in a beer tavern: "Jews not welcome." Germany, 1930s.

Above: *Der ewige Jude* (The Eternal Jew), poster for an exhibition in Munich. Germany, 1937.

Right: *Le Juif et la France* (The Jew and France), a poster by Michel Jacquot for an anti-semitic exhibition on Jews in occupied France.

Left: British Prime Minister Neville Chamberlain and German Chancellor Adolf Hitler at the signing of the peace agreement. Munich, Germany, September 30, 1938.

Inset: The Peace Agreement.

Above: Chamberlain during radio broadcast.

"This morning, the British Ambassador in Berlin handed the German Government a final note stating that unless we heard from them by 11 o'clock that they were prepared at once to withdraw their troops from Poland, a state of war would exist between us. I have to tell you now, that no such undertaking has been received, and that consequently this country is at war with Germany."
— Prime Minister Chamberlain September 1, 1939

Below: The New York Times front page. September 3, 1939.

We, the German Führer and Chancellor and the British Prime Minister, have had a further meeting today and are agreed in recognising that the question of Anglo-German relations is of the first importance for the two countries and for Europe.

We regard the agreement signed last night and the Anglo-German Naval Agreement as symbolic of the desire of our two peoples never to go to war with one another again.

We are resolved that the method of consultation shall be the method adopted to deal with any other questions that may concern our two countries, and we are determined to continue our efforts to remove possible sources of difference and thus to contribute to assure the peace of Europe.

Neville Chamberlain

September 30, 1938.

CHAMBERLAIN ANNOUNCES BRITAIN IS AT WAR WITH GERMANY

The New York Times.

BRITAIN AND FRANCE IN WAR AT 6 A. M.; HITLER WON'T HALT ATTACK ON POLES; CHAMBERLAIN CALLS EMPIRE TO FIGHT

Above: Blackout chart. The blackout began in England on September 1, 1939, and lasted until May 1945. Blackout regulations made it an offense to show a light during the hours of darkness in houses, businesses, all forms of transportation, and street lighting, thus making visibility of targets more difficult for enemy bombing attacks.

Above: Civilian Defense symbol. U.S.A.

Right: *Kannst Du das verantworten? Du hilfst dem Feind!* (Can you be responsible for this? You are helping the enemy!) Poster by Ludwig Hohlwein. Germany, 1942.

Left: Look Out in the Blackout, poster by Pat Keely. Great Britain.

Above: One of a number of Civil Defense leaflets issued by the British Government. 1939.

Above: Children hang the familiar blackout curtain in this game to foster blackout awareness. Great Britain, 1940s.

Right: Cigarette cards, which were included as a premium in cigarette packs, were very popular in pre-war England. At the outbreak of war, the cigarette companies issued this set of fifty cards on air raid precautions (A.R.P.) as a service to the general public.
ARNOLD SCHWARTZMAN

WILLS'S CIGARETTES

THE CIVILIAN RESPIRATOR—HOW TO REMOVE IT

WILLS'S CIGARETTES

THE CIVILIAN RESPIRATOR—HOW TO ADJUST IT

WILLS'S CIGARETTES

THE CIVILIAN DUTY RESPIRATOR

THE CIVILIAN RESPIRATOR—HOW TO ADJUST IT. Great care must be taken to see that the respirator is correctly fitted and adjusted, in order that a supply of pure air, quite free from gas, is ensured for breathing. The respirator is made so that it fits closely round the face, and is provided with adjustable straps to hold it in the correct position. It is important that the respirator be tried on and the straps properly adjusted to the requirements of the wearer (see picture), so that it may be put on at a moment's notice. (See also Cards Nos. 27 and 29). (No. 28)

THE CIVILIAN RESPIRATOR—HOW TO REMOVE IT. The picture shows the RIGHT way to take off a Civilian Respirator. This should be done by slipping the head harness forward from the back of the head. It is important that the respirator should be taken off in this way. The WRONG way to take it off is by taking hold of the metal box containing the filters and pulling the face-piece off the chin. By this method there is a danger of bending and cracking the transparent window. If this window is cracked, the respirator is useless. (No. 29)

A·R·P

THE CIVILIAN DUTY RESPIRATOR is of stronger construction than the Civilian Respirator (illustrated and described on Cards Nos. 27, 28 and 29) and is intended for those who might have to work in the presence of gas and could not go to a gas-protected refuge room. The respirator protects the eyes, nose, mouth and lungs against all known war gases. The face-piece is of moulded rubber, and the eye-pieces are of strong glass. There is an outlet valve opposite the nose; the protuberance at the side of the face-piece can be used to fit a microphone for speaking on the telephone. (No. 30)

Opposite: *Gas Mask*, painting by William Ramsden Brealey. Great Britain, 1939.
IMPERIAL WAR MUSEUM

Inset: An Air Raid Warden's armband. U.S.A.

WILLS'S CIGARETTES

EQUIPPING YOUR REFUGE ROOM—A

WILLS'S CIGARETTES

EQUIPPING YOUR REFUGE ROOM—B

Below: The A.R.P. badge was made of silver, as other metals were needed for the war effort.

WILLS'S CIGARETTES

A.R.P

AIR RAID PRECAUTIONS BADGE

"Women of Britain, give us your aluminium. We want it and we want it now.... We will turn your pots and pans into Spitfires and Hurricanes, Blenheims and Wellingtons. I ask therefore that everyone who has pots and pans, kettles and vacuum cleaners, hatpegs, coat-hangers, shoe-trees, bathroom fittings and household ornaments, cigarette boxes or any other articles made wholly or partly of aluminium, should hand them in at once to the local headquarters of the Women's Voluntary Services."
— *Lord Beaverbrook*

A million tons of metal railings were pulled from homes and public parks, however, the metal proved to be unsuitable for the war effort, and much of it was later jettisoned into the sea.

Right: Cigarette cards from a series entitled *Air-Raid Precautions*, shows (*above*) women forming a chain with canvas water buckets, and (*below*) women using a "two-men" portable manual fire-pump. Great Britain, 1939.

CHURCHMAN'S CIGARETTES

A CHAIN OF BUCKETS

CHURCHMAN'S CIGARETTES

TWO-MEN PORTABLE MANUAL FIRE-PUMP IN ACTION

Opposite: German civilians passing buckets of water to douse a fire after an Allied bombing attack. Berlin, Germany, 1943.
ULLSTEIN BILDERDIENST

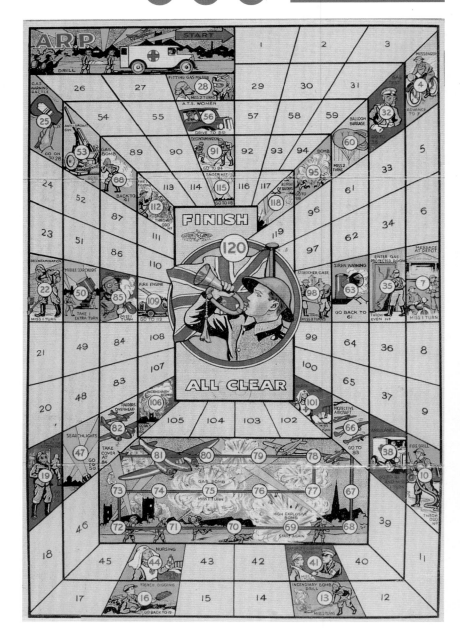

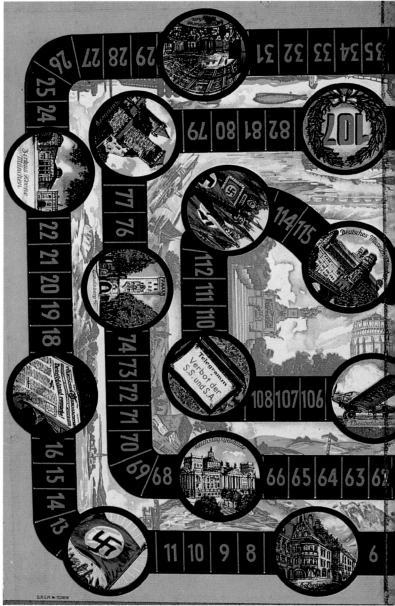

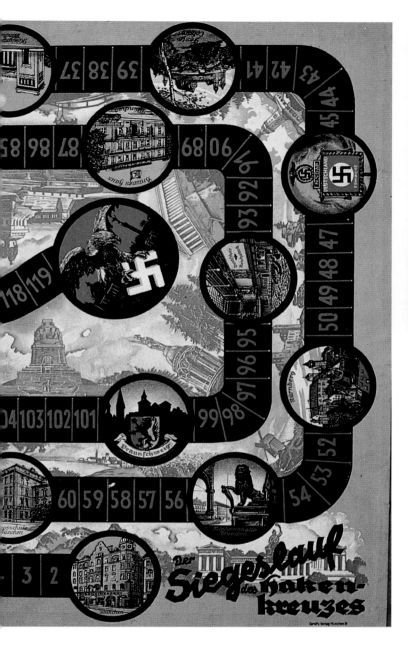

The Allied Supreme Command and the British MI5 (Military Intelligence) were perplexed by an amazing coincidence: just prior to D-Day, solutions to clues to the British Daily Telegraph crossword puzzles published on June 2, 1944, included the words: Overlord, Utah, Omaha, Mulberry, and Neptune—all code words selected for the Allied invasion.

Above: The Bomber, a WWII dexterity puzzle with a wartime theme. U.S.A., 1940s.
PHILIP COLLINS

Left: Der Siegeslauf des Hakenkreuzes (Victorious race of the swastika), Nazi board game. Germany, 1930s.

Far left: A.R.P. This board game illustrates the many activities of the A.R.P. warden, and some of the dangers they encountered. Great Britain, 1940s.

Right: British soldiers gather around the piano for a sing-a-along. Great Britain.
IMPERIAL WAR MUSEUM

Above: Sheet music: *Kiss Me Good-Night Sergeant-Major.* Great Britain, 1939.
© BRADBURY WOOD LTD.

Above: Sheet music: *Lili Marleen.* Germany, 1940.
© APOLLO VERLAG PAUL LINCKE, BERLIN

Right: The beer and food is lined up on the piano for this SS (Schutzstaffel: Protection Squad) banjo and accordion band. Germany.

As most German harmonicas and their boxes carried illustrations of the makers' factories which had been converted for munition production, an appeal was made to the British public to hand in these instruments to help identify the plants as targets for Allied bombing.

To bolster the morale of the troops stationed along the "Atlantic Wall," Field Marshal Rommel distributed approximately a hundred accordions to his men.

Possibly the most popular song of WWII was the German "Lili Marleen," which was later adopted by the Allied troops.

Left: Go by Shanks' Pony, poster by Lewitt – Him. Great Britain.
IMPERIAL WAR MUSEUM

Top left: Mound of victims' shoes at Auschwitz-Birkenau concentration camp, Poland.
SIMON WIESENTHAL CENTER

Bottom left: German soldiers trying on new boots.
ULLSTEIN BILDERDIENST

Right: "Keep 'em Flying," the U.S. Army Air Corps recruitment slogan, appeared on numerous items, such as matchbook covers, milk bottle tops, poster stamps, and decals. U.S.A., 1941.
TOMMY STEELE / ARNOLD SCHWARTZMAN

Above: Sheet music: *Johnny Zero.* U.S.A.. 1943;
© SANTLY-JOY INC.

Below: Sheet music: *Silver Wings In The Moonlight.* U.S.A., 1943.
© MILLER MUSIC CORPORATION

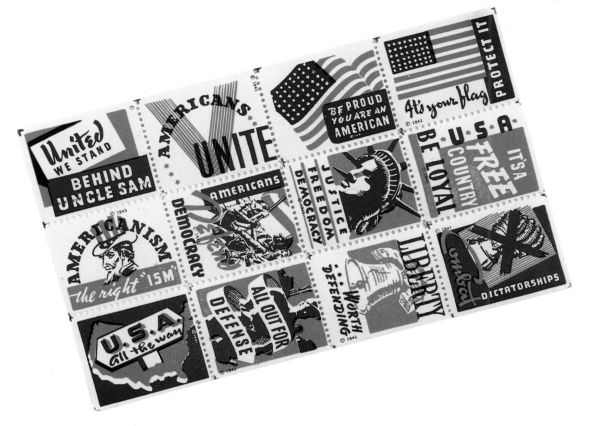

Sheets of poster stamps, for use on business and personal mail. U.S.A.

TOMMY STEELE

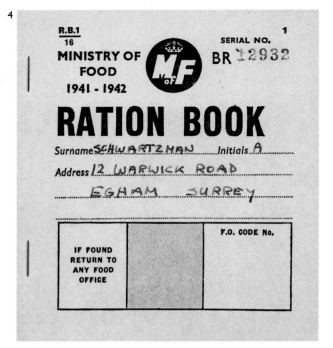

1/2: Press advertisements for
Cadbury chocolate.
The first, in Yiddish, from
The Jewish Times.
1929; and "Waiting for the
Day of Liberation."
Great Britain, 1940s.

3: *Dig On For Victory*, poster
by Peter Fraser.
Great Britain, 1940s.
IMPERIAL WAR MUSEUM

4: Food ration book.
Great Britain.

5: Symbol of the National
Victory Garden Institute.
U.S.A., 1942.

6: Poster: *Dig For Victory*.
Great Britain.
IMPERIAL WAR MUSEUM

7: "Utility mark". The Civilian
Clothing Order was a "no-frills"
production standard for clothing
and furniture.
Great Britain, June 1941.

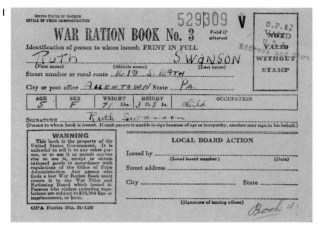

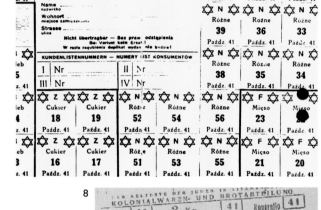

1/2: War Ration Book No. 3 cover, and page of ration stamps. U.S.A., 1940s.

3: Basic mileage ration card. U.S.A.

4: A blue fiber token, issued by the O.P.A. (Office of Price Administration) for processed foods. Red tokens were used for meats and fats. U.S.A.

5: Bread ration card. Germany.

6: Jewish ghetto food ration card. Poland, 1941.

7: 3 RM. (Reichsmark) S.S. garrison canteen, Buchenwald concentration camp. Germany.

8: Potato ration coupon, Lodz Ghetto, Poland.

9: Prisoners canteen coupon. Amersfoort Transit Camp, Netherlands, 1944.

10: Cholent bakery ticket. The Jewish dish made of meat, potatoes and beans was prepared on Fridays, and kept warm at the bakery until the Sabbath.

SIMON WIESENTHAL CENTER

Right: Your Talk May Kill Your Comrades, poster by Abram Games. Great Britain, 1942.

Above: Poster: *Feind hört mit!* (The enemy is listening!) Germany, 1943.

Above: Silence l'ennemi.. (Silence, the enemy listens to your secrets) poster by Paul Colin. France.

A FEW
CARELESS WORDS
MAY END IN THIS—

Many lives were lost in the last war through careless talk
Be on your guard! Don't discuss movements of ships or troops

Left: A Few Careless Words
May End in This —" poster by
Norman Wilkinson.
Great Britain.
IMPERIAL WAR MUSEUM

Above: Careless Talk Costs Lives,
one of a series of posters by
Fougasse (Cyril Kenneth Bird).
Great Britain, 1940.
IMPERIAL WAR MUSEUM

A set of five postcards depicting the Allied and Axis leaders:
1. Benito Mussolini
2. Joseph Stalin
3. Franklin D. Roosevelt
4. Adolf Hitler
5. Winston S. Churchill
Netherlands, 1945.
JOHN FROST HISTORIC NEWSPAPER SERVICE

Right: Decal:
There'll Always Be An England.
Canada, 1940s.
ARNOLD SCHWARTZMAN

Far right: Poster stamp:
There'll Always Be An England.
Canada, 1940s.
ARNOLD SCHWARTZMAN

THERE'LL ALWAYS
BE AN ENGLAND

"There'll Always Be An
ENGLAND"
"Carry On!" CHURCHILL
COPYRIGHT K40

Above: Jews were forced to build a wall surrounding the Warsaw Ghetto.
Poland, November 1940.

Left: Winston Churchill "the brick-layer" at his home, Chartwell, Kent, England.
IMPERIAL WAR MUSEUM

Far left: Adolf Hitler laying a foundation stone for a new building. Germany.

Above: Music sheet: *There'll Always Be An England*.
Great Britain, 1939.
© THE IRWIN DASH MUSIC CO. LTD.

Right: Young boy selling soap, and armbands which were compulsory for Jews. Warsaw Ghetto, 1940.
BUNDESARCHIV

The Judenstern (Jewish star) was compulsory to be worn by Jews in occupied Poland from 1939. This law was imposed on German Jews under the Nazi decree of September 1941.

Above: A blue Star of David on a white cloth armband from the Warsaw Ghetto.

Stars worn in occupied countries:
1. Germany; 2. France;
3. Netherlands; 4. Belgium;
5. Croatia; 6. Bulgaria.

1

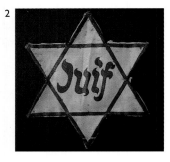

2

3

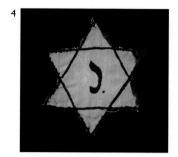

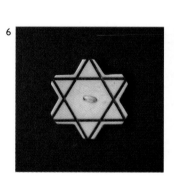

Left: An elderly woman wearing a yellow Star of David attached with a safety pin. Auschwitz-Birkenau, Poland.
BUNDESARCHIV

Above: A 20 Kronen note from Theresienstadt concentration camp. Terezin, Czechoslovakia.
SIMON WIESENTHAL CENTER

Above: An elderly man collapsed
on the sidewalk.
Warsaw Ghetto, 1940.
BUNDESARCHIV

Right: Governor Wächter's
edict for Jews aged twelve and
older to wear an identifying
armband on the right arm.
Krakow, Poland,
November 18, 1939.
SIMON WIESENTHAL CENTER

Opposite: A Jewish ghetto
policeman directing traffic
at a busy intersection.
Warsaw Ghetto, 1940.
BUNDESARCHIV

Der Distriktschef von Krakau

ANORDNUNG
Kennzeichnung der Juden im Distrikt Krakau

Ich ordne an, dass alle Juden im Alter von über 12 Jahren
im Distrikt Krakau mit Wirkung vom 1. 12. 1939 ausserhalb ihrer
eigenen Wohnung ein sichtbares Kennzeichen zu tragen haben. Dieser
Anordnung unterliegen auch nur vorübergehend im Distriktsbereich
anwesende Juden für die Dauer ihres Aufenthaltes.
Als Jude im Sinne dieser Anordnung gilt:

1. wer der mosaischen Glaubensgemeinschaft angehört oder angehört hat,
2. jeder, dessen Vater oder Mutter der mosaischen
Glaubensgemeinschaft angehört oder angehört hat.

Als Kennzeichen ist am rechten Oberarm der Kleidung und der
Überkleidung eine Armbinde zu tragen, die auf weissem Grunde
an der Aussenseite einen blauen Zionstern zeigt. Der weisse Grund
muss eine Breite von mindestens 10 cm. haben, der Zionstern muss
so gross sein, dass dessen gegenüberliegende Spitzen mindestens
8 cm. entfernt sind. Der Balken muss 1 cm. breit sein.
Juden, die dieser Verpflichtung nicht nachkommen, haben strenge Be-
strafung zu gewärtigen.
Für die Ausführung dieser Anordnung. Insbesondere die Versorgung
der Juden mit Kennzeichen, sind die Ältestenräte verantwortlich.

Krakau, den 18. 11. 1939.

gez. *Wächter*
Gouverneur

Left: Death by malnutrition and disease took its toll in the Warsaw Ghetto.
BUNDESARCHIV

Above: A bridge linking two parts of the Jewish ghetto, "Litzmannstadt." Lodz, Poland.
BUNDESARCHIV

Above: Obverse and reverse of a twenty and a one Reichsmark note. Lodz Ghetto, 1940.
SIMON WIESENTHAL CENTER

Right: Obverse and reverse of a five Mark coin. Lodz Ghetto, 1943.
SIMON WIESENTHAL CENTER

1/2: Poster stamps. U.S.A.

3: Sheet music: *Der Fuehrer's Face*. Donald Duck does his part for the war effort in the Walt Disney cartoon. U.S.A., 1942.
WALT DISNEY STUDIOS

4: *Adolf*, sheet music cover. Great Britain, 1939.
© LAWRENCE WRIGHT MUSIC PUBLISHERS

5: Film poster: *The Goose Steps Out*. Great Britain, 1942.
EALING STUDIOS

6: Record label: *Hitler's Funeral*. U.S.A.
© MUSICRAFT CORPORATION

7: Anti-Axis magazine advertisement. U.S.A.
JIM HEIMANN

8/9: Cover and inside of matchbook: "Strike At The Seat of Trouble." U.S.A.
TOMMY STEELE

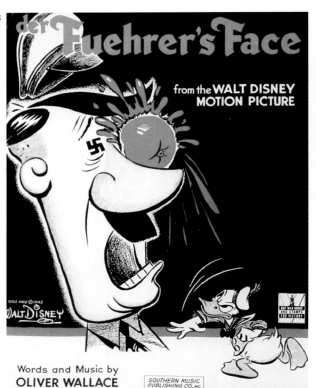

7

8

MATCH 'EM—
BOND FOR BOMB

*Strike at
the seat of
trouble*

**BUY
WAR BONDS**

OIL

is dandy

for

drowning

Greatest mystery of the war: "Where is the Luftwaffe?" Authorities say Germany has plenty of oil . . . BUT hasn't plenty of 100-octane gas. Many Axis planes have to use 60-octane. A neat little partnership of oil and coal improved America's position on 100-octane. To make, entirely from oil, the quantity of 100-octane fuel that American fighters need would have gobbled up enormous quantities of scarce metals. That's where coal came in. Coal is coked in Koppers ovens. The ovens recover much benzene. Combine benzene with propylene (an oil refinery product) and you get a compound with an octane blending rating of 132 and other properties desirable in aviation fuel. Americans add this to gasoline of say 70-octane and bring the whole mixture up to around 100.

Koppers also furnishes to the oil industry: plants for purifying gas . . . piston rings . . . self-aligning couplings . . . pressure-treated timbers, and other products.—Koppers Company and Affiliates, Pittsburgh, Pa.

Buy United States War Bonds and Stamps

KOPPERS
THE INDUSTRY THAT SERVES ALL INDUSTRY

9

STRIKE ON BACK SIDE

JU 88

JUNKERS FLUGZEUG- UND -MOTORENWERKE A.-G. DESSAU

Above and right: Two advertisements from the German military magazine *Signal*. 1941.

MERCEDES-BENZ

Above: Patriotic decals. U.S.A.
TOMMY STEELE

Above: Postage stamp:
"Win The War." U.S.A., 1942.

Left: Magazine advertisement
for the Douglas Aircraft
Company Inc.
JIM HEIMANN

Right: Glasgow L.M.S. Railway Home Guard Pipe Band provided a musical welcome to American soldiers who arrived in England.

IMPERIAL WAR MUSEUM   TOP18112

Above: Shoulder patch of the U.S. 4th Infantry Division, "Ivy."

A hit song of the period, "Mairzy Doats," included the lyrics: "Mairzy Doats and dozy doats and liddle lamzy divey... If the words sound queer, and funny to your ear, Sing 'Mares eat oats and does eat oats and little lambs eat ivy.'"

© 1943 MILLER MUSIC CORP.

Left: A platoon of Black G.I.s "jazz march" along a typical British main street.
IMPERIAL WAR MUSEUM

A story in the New Statesman related how a grand English lady, wishing to do her part towards the war effort, wrote to the Commanding Officer of the local U.S. base to invite half a dozen of his men to Sunday lunch. She added to the invitation, "No Jews, please." On the appointed day, the hostess opened the door to welcome her guests. Standing before her were six black G.I.s. Horrified, she exclaimed, "There must be some mistake." "Oh, no Ma'am," one of the soldiers replied. "Colonel Cohen never makes mistakes."

Above: Record album notes of Irving Berlin's All Soldier Show: *This Is The Army.*
U.S.A., 1942.
DECCA RECORD INC.

Far right: Captain Glenn Miller and the Army Air Force Band at the "Stage Door Canteen." "Somewhere in England," 1944.

Right: Shoulder patch for the A.F.N. (American Forces Network). U.S.A.

Right: German military band entertains munitions factory workers during a break.
ULLSTEIN BILDERDIENST

Above and below: Posters for E.N.S.A. (Entertainments National Service Association—affectionately known as "Every Night Something Awful"), founded in 1941. Great Britain.

Left: Bing Crosby entertains the troops at a U.S.O. (United Service Organizations) show. "somewhere in Europe."
ULLSTEIN BILDERDIENST

Above: Postage stamp: "Women in our Armed Services." Represented are, from left, Marines, Army, Navy, and Air Corps. U.S.A., 1952

Over 300,000 women served in the U.S. Armed Forces during WWII as W.A.C.S.: Women's Army Air Corps; W.A.S.P.S.: Women Air Force Service Pilots; and W.A.V.E.S.: Women Accepted for Voluntary Emergency Service.

Right: U.S. nurses training in England for the second front. Their job was to follow the troops of liberation and establish hospital units. 1944.
IMPERIAL WAR MUSEUM   NYT21630

Inset: Poster: *My Girl's a WOW* (Woman Ordinance Worker). U.S.A.
IMPERIAL WAR MUSEUM

Above: Ruby Loftus Screwing a Breech-ring, painting of a munitions worker by Dame Laura Knight. Great Britain.
IMPERIAL WAR MUSEUM

Left: Join the ATS (Auxilliary Territorial Services). After its appearance, the poster was banned by the British Parliament, which deemed the poster "unsuitable" as the image was considered to be too glamorous. Abram Games.
Great Britain, 1941.
IMPERIAL WAR MUSEUM

Right: Film poster: *1944 Year of Decision*, designed by Mayo for the National Film Board of Canada. 1944.

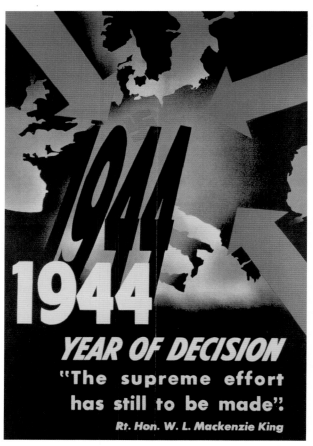

1944

1944

YEAR OF DECISION

"The supreme effort has still to be made".

Rt. Hon. W. L. Mackenzie King

"Mrs. Miniver" is propaganda worth a hundred battleships."
— Winston Churchill's comment on the patriotic 1942 film.

"D-Day! Tuesday, June 6.
Seems a little queer to go to a movie here in camp tonight just as if nothing had happened. Jack and Arlie and I talked about whether we ought to go. It seemed somehow disrespectful. Loftis finally said, "Hell, let's make the most of what we've got while we've got it. We can't do any good by not going, and we'll be over there next."

It was an Abbott and Costello comedy and I don't suppose any of us ever laughed harder. Came out feeling pretty good, but it soon wore off. Tent is full tonight, everybody guessing when we'll go, too excited about the events of the day to settle down. It's hit me differently. I feel awfully tired, as if I had worked hard all day. It's the let-down, I suppose."

— The Journal of G.I. Sergeant Giles

Opposite: Postage stamp celebrating the 50th anniversary of motion pictures. U.S.A., 1945.

Inset: A publicity still from *Buck Privates* (1940), starring Bud Abbott and Lou Costello.
COURTESY OF THE ACADEMY OF MOTION PICTURE ARTS AND SCIENCES

UNITED

3¢

POSTAGE

STATES OF AMERICA

TH ANNIVERSARY OF MOTION PICTURES

Right: Take Off painting of the interior of a bomber by Dame Laura Knight. Great Britain, 1944.
IMPERIAL WAR MUSEUM

Right: Cigarette card: Air defense control room. Great Britain, 1939.

CHURCHMAN'S CIGARETTES

REPRESENTATION OF AIR DEFENCE CONTROL ROOM

Opposite: Headquarters Room, plotting the Overlord Operation at Southwick House, near Portsmouth. Painting by Barnet Freedman. Great Britain, 1944.
IMPERIAL WAR MUSEUM

Right: Members of Britain's Royal Corps of Signals examine their "invasion currency."

Above: French "invasion currency" issued to troops.

Left: Allied "invasion" Marks issued to the troops for use in Germany.
SIMON WIESENTHAL CENTER

Above: Allied Military Authority Schillings issued to the Allied troops in Austria.
SIMON WIESENTHAL CENTER

Right: Players Navy Cut and (*center*) Woodbine, two British brands of cigarettes, which were popular with the troops. 1940s.

Far right: Salem No. 6, "Turkish" cigarette packet. Germany, 1940s.

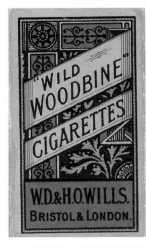

Right: American G.I.s enjoy a Lucky Strike before hitting the Normandy beaches. June 6, 1944.

Above: Advertisement for Lucky Strike cigarettes. "Luckies" changed their predominantly green pack to white, as the green printing ink contained metal required for the war effort. U.S.A., 1942.

the SUCCESS of DEFENSE is up to YOU

Keep the Defense Line STRONG

STEP ON IT

CRUSH THE AXIS

PRESERVE FREEDOM

INVEST IN WAR BONDS AND STAMPS

HOLLYWOOD 27, CALIF.

It's up to Us

to KEEP 'EM FIRING

61

Left: The Second World War brought about a plethora of patriotic themes to illustrate matchbook covers. U.S.A., 1940s.
JIM HEIMANN / TOMMY STEELE

"Invasion June 6th 1944.

Mrs. Rothwell (maid) came in to us at Breakfast Time, all breathless, to say she had heard Eisenhower over wireless say that Invasion had begun.

We thought she might have misheard. Went out on bicycle. A soldier in charge of a lorry asked me where he could buy cigarettes "not at a Pub—because we musn't drink to-day".

In the evening saw glider after glider being towed slowly and steadily towards coast. All the northern skies full of them— imagine them full of troops Then I knew Invasion had really started."

— Extract from the diary of Miss H. A. Harrison
IMPERIAL WAR MUSEUM

CLOSE COVER BEFORE STRIKING

Coronado, Calif.

U.S. NAVAL AMPHIBIOUS TRAINING BASE

ONE Force ★ ONE Fight ★ ONE Foe

THEY ASKED FOR IT!

LET 'EM HAVE IT!

For the Nation

HOLD THAT LINE

MADE IN U.S.A.

UNITED STATES NAVY

Above: Rebus of Churchill's cigar, Roosevelt's cigarette holder, and Stalin's pipe.

Above: U.S. Generals at S.H.A.E.F. (Supreme Headquarters Allied Expeditionary Force) headquarters in Versailles, France.

Front row from left:
Generals William H. Simpson,
George S. Patton,
Carl A. Spaatz,
Dwight D. Eisenhower,
Omar N. Bradley,
Courtney Hodges,
Leonard Gerow;

Back row from left:
Stearley,
Hoyt S. Vandenberg,
Walter Bedell Smith,
Otto P. Weyland,
Nugent.

France, May 1945.
ULLSTEIN BILDERDIENST

Right: The D-Day landing beaches: Utah, Omaha (U.S.A.), and Gold, Juno, and Sword (Great Britain).

UTAH OMAHA GOLD JUNO SWORD

Lieutenant General Omar Bradley

Admiral Sir Bertram Ramsay

Air Chief Marshal Sir Arthur Tedder

Supreme Commander General
Dwight D. Eisenhower

General
Sir Bernard L. Montgomery

Air Marshall
Sir Trafford Leigh-Mallory

Lieutenant General
Walter Bedell Smith

Above: S.H.A.E.F. shoulder patch.

Above: Plaque commemorating Eisenhower's first S.H.A.E.F. headquarters, Norfolk House, St. James's Square, London.
PHOTOGRAPH: ARNOLD SCHWARTZMAN

Left: The Allied Commanders at the S.H.A.E.F. headquarters prior to D-Day.
England, June 1944.
POPPERFOTO

Right: British paratroopers being briefed before takeoff. These "pathfinders" were the first men to land in France; their job was to direct other airborne forces in. June 5, 1944.
IMPERIAL WAR MUSEUM   H39089

Above: "Pegasus" Insignia of the British Airborne Division.

The Lord gave David victory everywhere he went. CHRONICLES 18:6

Left: On the eve of the D-Day invasion, General Dwight David Eisenhower gives a pep-talk to paratroopers of the US 101st Airborne Division, their faces camouflaged, before departing from their base in Greenham Common, Newbury, England.
NATIONAL ARCHIVES

Above: Shoulder patch of the U.S. 101st Airborne Division "Screaming Eagles".

Above: General Eisenhower's diary entry. June 5, 1944.

Right: General Eisenhower's letter distributed to all soldiers, sailors, and airmen as the invasion was under way.

Above: Let 'em Have It, Buy Extra Bonds, poster for the 4th war loan, by Bernard Perlin. U.S.A., 1943

SUPREME HEADQUARTERS
ALLIED EXPEDITIONARY FORCE

Soldiers, Sailors and Airmen of the Allied Expeditionary Force!

You are about to embark upon the Great Crusade, toward which we have striven these many months. The eyes of the world are upon you. The hopes and prayers of liberty-loving people everywhere march with you. In company with our brave Allies and brothers-in-arms on other Fronts, you will bring about the destruction of the German war machine, the elimination of Nazi tyranny over the oppressed peoples of Europe, and security for ourselves in a free world.

Your task will not be an easy one. Your enemy is well trained, well equipped and battle-hardened. He will fight savagely.

But this is the year 1944! Much has happened since the Nazi triumphs of 1940-41. The United Nations have inflicted upon the Germans great defeats, in open battle, man-to-man. Our air offensive has seriously reduced their strength in the air and their capacity to wage war on the ground. Our Home Fronts have given us an overwhelming superiority in weapons and munitions of war, and placed at our disposal great reserves of trained fighting men. The tide has turned! The free men of the world are marching together to Victory!

I have full confidence in your courage, devotion to duty and skill in battle. We will accept nothing less than full Victory!

Good Luck! And let us all beseech the blessing of Almighty God upon this great and noble undertaking.

Dwight Eisenhower

Right: Postage stamp commemorating the twentieth anniversary of the liberation of France. 1964.

Opposite: U.S. troops approach the Normandy beaches. June 6, 1944.

NATIONAL ARCHIVES

Right: "Invasion!"
Los Angeles Times.
Tuesday, June 6, 1944.

Above: Shoulder patch of the
U.S. 1st Infantry Division,
"The Big Red One."

Opposite: U.S. troops hit
Omaha Beach. June 6, 1944.
NATIONAL ARCHIVES

"*This is D-Day…the invasion has begun. The English gave the news at 8 o'clock this morning…seems too wonderful…seems like a fairy tale and, Kitty, the best part of the invasion is that I have the feeling that friends are approaching…we have been oppressed by those terrible Germans for so long…that the thought of friends and delivery fills us with confidence…now it doesn't concern the Jews anymore. No, it concerns Holland and all of occupied Europe.*

Perhaps, Margot says, I may yet be able to go back to school in September or October.

Yours, Anne."

— *Diary of Anne Frank, June 6, 1944*

Right: *Life* D-Day issue, which included the Robert Capa Normandy landing photograph. June 19, 1944.

Opposite: An American G.I. comes ashore H-Hour, 06:30, Omaha Beach, Normandy. June 6, 1944.
ROBERT CAPA–MAGNUM

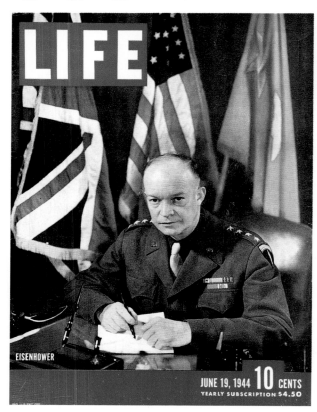

"I need ketchup and mayonnaise …those small boxes of Altman's have begun to arrive. They really hit the spot. Please order another set. Also, would you send me Life magazine with the story of the invasion in it."
— A G.I's letter sent home from Normandy.

"The water was cold, and the beach still more than a hundred yards away. The bullets tore holes in the water around me, and I made for the nearest steel obstacle. A soldier got there at the same time, and for a few minutes we shared its cover. He took the waterproofing off his rifle and began to shoot without much aiming at the smoke-hidden beach. The sound of his rifle gave him enough courage to move forward and he left the obstacle to me. It was a foot larger now, and I felt safe enough to take pictures of the other guys hiding just like I was."
— Robert Capa

TU Y CROIS ENCORE AU DÉBARQUEMENT, TOI ?

GELOOF GIJ NOG AAN EEN LANDING .. ?

YOU STILL BELIEVE THEY WILL . . . .

. . . LAND OVER HERE ?

Above: Poster: *Invasion!* Great Britain, 1944.
IMPERIAL WAR MUSEUM

Above: Shoulder patch of the British I Corps.

Above left: One of a series of liberation postcards. Belgium, 1944.

Left: Decal: "Between Us We Can Do The Job." Canada.

Left: British Royal Marine Commandos wade ashore. Juno Beach, St. Aubin sur Mer. Normandy, June 6, 1944.
IMPERIAL WAR MUSEUM   B5218

71

Right: *This Is The Year*, poster by Clive Upton. Great Britain.
IMPERIAL WAR MUSEUM

Right: Detail of a stained glass window commemorating D-Day. Portsmouth Cathedral, England.
PHOTOGRAPH: ARNOLD SCHWARTZMAN

Right: Shoulder patch of the British 2nd Army.

Opposite: British casualties on Sword Beach, La Breche, exposed to heavy mortar and machine gun fire. Normandy, June 6, 1944.
IMPERIAL WAR MUSEUM   B5114

19. - BERNIÈRES (Calvados). — La Plage

Left: Let's Go...Canada!
Poster by Eveleigh.
MINISTRY OF PUBLIC INFORMATION CANADA

Above: King George VI postage
stamp and V···− cachet. Canada.

Above: Commemorative stamp.
Liberation of France.

Opposite: Canadian troops of the
North Nova Scotia Highlanders
and Highland Light Infantry,
some carrying bicycles, wade
ashore at Juno Beach, Bernières,
Normandy. June 6, 1944.
IMPERIAL WAR MUSEUM   A23938

Inset: Postcard shows holiday-
makers in a canoe "invading" the
beach at Bernières in an earlier
peaceful time.

Troops of the British 13/18th Hussars, with blackened faces, crouch low as they wait to move forward after landing on the Normandy beaches, June 6, 1944.
IMPERIAL WAR MUSEUM   B5090

Left: *The Evening News.*
Great Britain, June 6, 1944.

Above: Stained glass D-Day
memorial window, unveiled by
Her Majesty Queen Elizabeth
The Queen Mother.
Portsmouth Cathedral, Great
Britain. June 6, 1984.

PHOTOGRAPH: ARNOLD SCHWARTZMAN

Left: A film scene identification
slate, held by British cameraman
Sgt Leatherbarrow.
Normandy, June 6, 1944.

IMPERIAL WAR MUSEUM

Opposite: Wounded British
soldiers on the beach
awaiting evacuation.

IMPERIAL WAR MUSEUM

Right: Prisoners are taken as troops of the U.S. 2nd Ranger Battalion occupy a German battery at Pointe du Hoc.
U.S. flag acts as marker to prevent Allied bombardment.
NATIONAL ARCHIVES

Inset: A "Safe Conduct" pass assured Germans that if they surrendered they would be given fair treatment.
SIMON WIESENTHAL CENTER

"They're murdering us here. Let's move inland and get murdered."
— Colonel Charles D. Canham

"Two kinds of people are staying on this beach, the dead and those who are going to die. Now let's get the hell out of here."
— Colonel George A. Taylor

Opposite: Painting:
Le Bec du Hoc, Grandchamp.
by French impressionist
Georges Seurat.
France, 1885.
TATE GALLERY / ART RESOURCE

Right: General Montgomery.
Normandy, June 11, 1944.
IMPERIAL WAR MUSEUM   B5337

Above: Insignia of the British
21st Army Group, worn
by General Montgomery.

Above: A personal message from
General Montgomery to the
British troops.
IMPERIAL WAR MUSEUM

Above: Shoulder patch of the U.S. First Army.

Above: Poster stamps. 1942.

Right: His Majesty King George VI and General Montgomery walking along the beach near Courseulles. Normandy, June 16, 1944.
IMPERIAL WAR MUSEUM   B5613

Above: General Montgomery talking with French fishermen, Port-en-Bessin. Normandy, June 10, 1944.
IMPERIAL WAR MUSEUM   B5318

Prior to D-Day, British General Alan Brooke, Chief of the Imperial General Staff, remarked to King George VI that Montgomery was "a very good soldier, but I think he is after my job," to which the King replied "I thought he was after mine."

Above: "Hobart's Funnies." The Bobbin tank, one of many ingenious devices invented by Major General Percy Hobart (General Montgomery's brother-in-law), could lay a ten-foot wide canvas path across sand for vehicles. Great Britain.
IMPERIAL WAR MUSEUM   H37886

"*We shall go unto the end, we shall fight in France, we shall fight on the seas and the oceans, we shall fight with growing confidence, and growing strength in the air, we shall defend our island, whatever the cost may be, we shall fight on the beaches, we shall fight on the landing grounds, we shall fight in the fields and in the streets, we shall fight in the hills; we shall never surrender…*"

—*Winston Churchill*
June 4, 1940
House of Commons
Great Britain

Above: WWI postcard.
Great Britain.

Right: American troops coming
ashore, Normandy, 1944.
IMPERIAL WAR MUSEUM   PL26128

Inset: Turn of the century
bathers at Deauville, Normandy.

*Following an appeal on the
British Broadcasting Corporation,
listeners sent ten million postcards
of the Normandy coastline,
which were used by the invasion
planners to identify the
D-Day landing sites.*

Above: Postage stamp
commemorating the 30th
anniversary of the Normandy
invasion. France 1974.

Above: Sheet music:
Somewhere In France.
U.S.A., 1917.
© M. WITMARK & SONS

374 DEAUVILLE. — *La Baigneuse à l'Aigrette.* — LL.

Above: Guidebook *How to See Paris* issued to the soldiers of the Allied Armies.

Right: A patriotic banner hangs in the window of a Jewish religious goods shop on Broom Street, New York, 1942.
LIBRARY OF CONGRESS

Above: *God Bless America* by Irving Berlin, sung by Bing Crosby.
DECCA RECORDS INC.

Above: Matchbook cover. U.S.A., 1940s.
TOMMY STEELE

"...the wretched refuse of your teeming shore, send these, the homeless, tempest-tost to me, I lift my lamp beside the Golden Door!"
— *Emma Lazarus, 1848–1887*

Above: America opens its "Golden Door" to a new wave of immigrants. Lithographic "scrap." U.S.A., 1909.
HEBREW PUBLISHING COMPANY

Above: Poster stamp: *Boycott Hitler!* U.S.A.

Left: D-Day service in a synagogue on West 23rd Street, New York. June 6, 1944
LIBRARY OF CONGRESS

Right: The first live broadcast from the Normandy beachhead took place on Sunday, June 18, when William Downs (CBS) (*right*) and Frank Gillard (BBC) (*below*) operating from a Royal Signals truck just off the beaches, transmitted messages for their respective systems. Gillard's message, which was heard on the 9 o'clock news, is claimed to be the first direct BBC transmission from Normandy.

IMPERIAL WAR MUSEUM   B5793   B5792

Far right: A French civilian has produced his radio and listens to the latest news bulletin, with two British soldiers.

IMPERIAL WAR MUSEUM   B5026

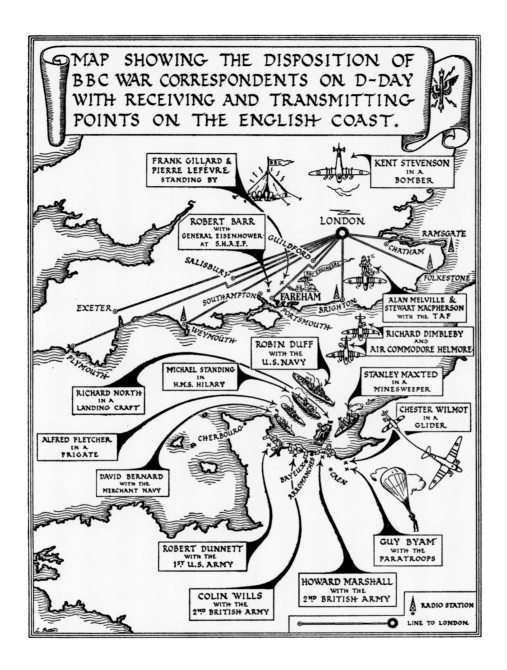

Left: Map showing the locations of BBC war correspondents on D-Day.
BRITISH BROADCASTING CORPORATION

Above: Dust jacket of the British Broadcasting Corporation's Year Book for 1944, which marked 21 years of day to day broadcasting. Great Britain, 1944.
BBC PUBLICATIONS

Left: American servicemen listening to news of the Allied advance in Europe, *and below*: at the American Red Cross "Rainbow Corner," Piccadilly, London.
NATIONAL ARCHIVES

Opposite: U.S. servicemen tune in to the latest news from the Front.
NATIONAL ARCHIVES

Left: Cover of *Lilliput*, by Trier. This popular wartime British magazine, as well as *Weekly Illustrated* and *Picture Post*, was created by Stefan Lorant, a German refugee. Great Britain.

Right: German servicemen tune in to the news in their mess hall.
SIMON WIESENTHAL CENTER

Above: Poster: *Ganz Deutschland hört den Führer mit dem Volksempfänger.* (All of Germany listens to the Führer with the people's radio.)
Germany, 1930s.
SIMON WIESENTHAL CENTER

Above: Press advertisement for Philips All-Wave Receiver. Great Britain.

Above: Sergeant Stokes, a master cook in the British Army Catering Corps, prepares the day's menu. April 20, 1944 (Hitler's birthday).
IMPERIAL WAR MUSEUM   B5832

Above: Sheet music: *Somewhere In France With You.* Great Britain.
© PETER MAURICE MUSIC CO. LTD

Right: British troops enjoy a cup of tea at the newly-opened N.A.A.F.I. (Navy, Army, and Air Force Institutes) canteen, previously a florist shop. Caen, France, 1944.
IMPERIAL WAR MUSEUM   B7895

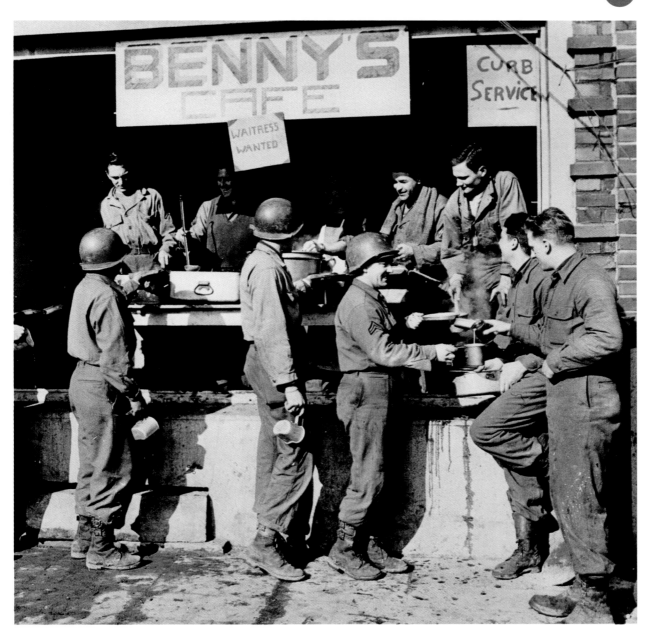

Left: "Bennys Cafe," a makeshift U.S. army cafe in a partially destroyed house. "Somewhere in France," 1945.
ULLSTEIN BILDERDIENST

Above: Shoulder patch of the U.S. 3rd Armored Division.

Above: Shoulder patch of the U.S. VII Corps.

Above: Two "Victory" covers. On the lower envelope, the initial "B" in the recipient's name was a family code indicating the sender was stationed in Bristol, England. U.S.A., 1943.

ARNOLD SCHWARTZMAN

Right: V···—Mail letters sent home by Private Ralph Levine.

SIMON WIESENTHAL CENTER

Left: During a quiet moment near the front line, a member of the British Second Essex Regiment writes a letter home. Normandy, June 1944.
IMPERIAL WAR MUSEUM   B5533

Above: Sheet music: *Wait For Me Mary*. U.S.A., 1942.
© REMICK MUSIC CORPORATION

Above: Sheet music: *We"ll Meet Again*. Great Britain, 1939.
© THE IRWIN DASH MUSIC CO. LTD

Right: British troops of the 6th Green Howards set up headquarters complete with a mailbox.
Normandy, August 1944.
IMPERIAL WAR MUSEUM B8679

Above: German children writing to their fathers at the Front.
ULLSTEIN BILDERDIENST

Above: Hitler Youth sorting the mail. Germany.
ULLSTEIN BILDERDIENST

Left: British troops of the Royal
Tank Regiment in Normandy
receiving their first mail since
their arrival in France.
IMPERIAL WAR MUSEUM   B5463

Above: "Charging Boar" insignia
of British XXX Corps.

Above: A young German mail
carrier delivering a package to a
bomb damaged house. 1944.
ULLSTEIN BILDERDIENST

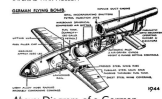

Above: *A Flying Bomb Over Tower Bridge*, painting by Frederick T. W. Cook. Great Britain, 1944.
IMPERIAL WAR MUSEUM

Above: Diagram of a German V-1 Flying Bomb. Great Britain, 1944.
IMPERIAL WAR MUSEUM

Left: A Jewish congregation takes shelter during a bomb attack on London. Great Britain, 1940s.
IMPERIAL WAR MUSEUM

Opposite: *V-1 Bomb*, painting by Leslie Cole. Great Britain.
IMPERIAL WAR MUSEUM

Right: A band of French WWI veterans welcomes the liberating troops parading through the streets of Paris, 1944.
NATIONAL ARCHIVES

Above: Postcard: *V France.* A cockerel, the national symbol of France, is incorporated into the "V" for victory. France, 1945.

Opposite: General Charles de Gaulle walking through the streets of Bayeux followed by a crowd of enthusiastic citizens. Normandy, June 14, 1944.
IMPERIAL WAR MUSEUM B5481

Right: "We are all alive" –
Families have left messages and
forwarding addresses on the
ruins of their bombed-out
apartment building. Berlin, 1945.
ULLSTEIN BILDERDIENST

Above: Orange box label:
" *Battle Front*,"
California, U.S.A., 1940s.

Opposite: White flags of truce
were hung from balconies as
American troops marched
through a bomb damaged city
on their advance to Berlin.
Germany, Spring 1945.
ULLSTEIN BILDERDIENST

Right: Allied troops are greeted by jubilant crowds waving white flags of truce. Munich, Germany, May 1945.
ULLSTEIN BILDERDIENST

Above: Postcard: *Vive la Libération!* (Long live the liberation!). Belgium, 1945.

Opposite: German Villagers Waving White Flags at the approach of Our Tanks. Drawing by Edward Ardizzone. Great Britain, 1945.
IMPERIAL WAR MUSEUM

Right: Russian, American, and British soldiers on the balcony of the destroyed Reichskanzlei (Chancellory) building. Berlin, 1945.
ULLSTEIN BILDERDIENST

Above: *Victorious Yank.* *Life* magazine. May 14, 1945.

Inset: Postcard: *Right is Might...* Belgium, 1945.

L'UNION FAIT LA FORCE . . .
EENDRACHT MAAKT MACHT . . . .
RIGHT IS MIGHT . . . .

Above: Poster: *We Will Raise The Flag of Victory Over Berlin*, by Viktor Ivanov. U.S.S.R., 1944.

Above: A class of school children reading the latest news of the war. Germany, 1940.
ULLSTEIN BILDERDIENST

Right: Newspaper headline reads: Atlantic wall has been breached in several places. Germany, June 6, 1944.

Right: Hitler Youth "newspaper boys" distributing copies of a German newspaper.
ULLSTEIN BILDERDIENST

Left: German ex-prisoners of war
and civilians reading a newspaper
printed under the Allied Military
Government, giving full details of
the end of the war.
Germany, May 9, 1945.
ROBERT HUNT LIBRARY

Above: *Der Krieg ist vorüber!*
(The war is over), headline from
the *Hamburger Nachrichten-Blatt.*
Germany, May 9, 1945.
JOHN FROST HISTORIC NEWSPAPER SERVICE

Right: "EXTRA! V-E DAY!
Nazis surrender unconditionally
to Allied powers."
Los Angeles Times, May 7, 1945.

Opposite: A sea of American
flags heralds the news that
"Germany surrenders."
U.S.A., May 7, 1945.
NATIONAL ARCHIVES

Pages 120/121: "War Is Over."
Sailors and civilians display
newspaper banner headlines.
U.S.A., May 7, 1945.
NATIONAL ARCHIVES

Above: Poster stamps:
The 5th Column. U.S.A.
TOMMY STEELE

Right: Tablecloth: *Score Board,*
Allies v. Axis. U.S.A.
JIM HEIMANN

Left: Dexterity puzzle:
Keep 'em Rolling For Victory.
PHILIP COLLINS

Above: "Victory" decals.
JIM HEIMANN / TOMMY STEELE

Right: "Victory" poster stamps. Canada and U.S.A.
TOMMY STEELE / ARNOLD SCHWARTZMAN

" La Gazette Officielle "

REWARD OF £25

A REWARD OF £25 WILL BE GIVEN TO THE PERSON WHO FIRST GIVES TO THE INSPECTOR OF POLICE INFORMATION LEADING TO THE CONVICTION OF ANYONE (NOT ALREADY DISCOVERED) FOR THE OFFENCE OF MARKING ON ANY GATE, WALL OR OTHER PLACE WHATSOEVER VISIBLE TO THE PUBLIC THE LETTER "V" OR ANY OTHER SIGN OR ANY WORD OR WORDS CALCULATED TO OFFEND THE GERMAN AUTHORITIES OR SOLDIERS

THIS 8th DAY OF JULY, 1941
VICTOR G CAREY,
Bailiff.

Above: Reward notice for information leading to the arrest of anyone making the "V" sign. German occupied British Channel Islands. 1941.

JOIN A "VICTORY V" CLUB

Above: Newspaper advertisement. Great Britain, 1940s.

Opposite: Two "Victory" flower vases. U.S.A.
HENRY VIZCARRA

"V for Victory" postcards.
U.S.A., 1941.
ARNOLD SCHWARTZMAN

Right: Prime Minister
Winston Churchill greets the
people with his famous "V" sign
outside No. 10 Downing Street,
London, May 8, 1945.
IMPERIAL WAR MUSEUM   HU55521

*This is your victory, it is no
victory of a party or of any class,
it is a victory of the great British
nation as a whole. We were all
alone for a whole year. Did anyone want to give in? Were we
down-hearted? The lights went
out and the bombs came down.
But every man, woman, and
child in this country had no
thought of quitting the struggle.
London could take it. So we came
back after long months, back
from the jaws of death, out of the
mouth of hell, while all the
world wondered. All over the
world, wherever the bird of
freedom chirps in human hearts,
people will look back to what we
have done and say: 'don't
despair. Don't yield to violence
and tyranny. March straight
forward and die, if need be,
unconquered'.*
— Winston S. Churchill

Opposite: Churchill, surrounded
by exuberant crowds, as he
travels triumphantly along
Whitehall to the Houses of
Parliament, after giving his
V-E Day speech. London, 1945.
IMPERIAL WAR MUSEUM   SG45955

Right: "V-E Day—It's All Over."
Daily Mail.
Great Britain, May 8, 1945.

Opposite: Thousands crowd into Piccadilly Circus to celebrate the Allies' victory in Europe. At right of picture, American flags hang outside the U.S. Red Cross "Rainbow Corner," a favorite venue for American forces in England. May 8, 1945.
NATIONAL ARCHIVES

Right: Picture Post
"Victory Special."
Great Britain, May 19, 1945.
JOHN FROST HISTORIC NEWSPAPER SERVICE

Above: Vict'ry Polka, a popular
WWII song by (British born)
Jule Styne and Sammy Cahn,
performed by Bing Crosby and
the Andrews Sisters. U.S.A.
DECCA RECORD INC

Above: Victory stamp with
symbols of peace and
reconstruction.
Great Britain, 1946.

Opposite: Crowds dancing in the
streets to celebrate V-E Day.
London, May 8, 1945.
NATIONAL ARCHIVES

…My parents went out on the balcony in response to the huge crowds outside. I think we went on the balcony nearly every hour…my sister and I realized we couldn't see what the crowds were enjoying. My mother had put her tiara on for the occasion, so we asked my parents if we could go out and see for ourselves. I remember we were terrified of being recognized so I pulled my uniform cap well down over my eyes….We cheered the King and Queen on the balcony and then walked miles through the streets. I remember lines of unknown people linking arms and walking down Whitehall, all of us just swept along on a tide of happiness and relief….After crossing Green Park we stood outside and shouted "We want the King," and we were successful in seeing my parents on the balcony, having cheated slightly because we sent a message into the house to say we were waiting outside. I think it was one of the most memorable nights of my life.

— Queen Elizabeth II, from the BBC documentary:
The Way We Were, *Radio 4, May 8, 1985.*

BRITISH BROADCASTING CORPORATION

Right: Postage stamp:
Victorious American troops
march down the Champs
Élysées, Paris, France.
U.S.A., 1945.

Below: Postcard: Horse drawn
traffic along the Champs Élysées.
1900s.

I   PARIS. — L'Arc-de-Triomphe et les Champs-Élysées. — LL.

Right: Postage stamp
commemorating the
twentieth anniversary of
the liberation of France. 1964.

Opposite: Parisians and their
liberators celebrate V-E Day
on Place de l'Opera.
NATIONAL ARCHIVES

Right: The "Yanks" provided much fodder for cartoonists in war-time Britain, such as Giles.

In 1946, when Field Marshal Montgomery visited California, Hollywood movie mogul Sam Goldwyn gave a dinner for the British war hero. Goldwyn, introducing him, said: "It gives me great pleasure to welcome to Hollywood a very distinguished soldier. Ladies and gentlemen, I propose a toast to Marshall Field Montgomery."

The silence was broken by Jack Warner: "Montgomery Ward, you mean."

(Marshall Field and Montgomery Ward are American department stores.)

Opposite: Cartoon by David Low: *The Nightmare Passes.* Great Britain, 1945.

"I don't care if the war is nearly over—I'm not selling my cab for a fiver for a souvenir."

Left and opposite: Liberation postcards: Netherlands and Belgium. 1945.
ARNOLD SCHWARTZMAN

Right: Poster for the U.S. Treasury Department: *Hasten The Homecoming,* by Norman Rockwell, taken from his *Saturday Evening Post* cover of May 26, 1945
NATIONAL ARCHIVES

Above: A "Welcome Home" banner. U.S.A., 1945.
ROBERT HUNT LIBRARY

Left: An exuberant welcome for a "liberator." "Somewhere in France," 1944.
NATIONAL ARCHIVES

Above: Poster: *Come Into The Factories.* England, c. 1942.
IMPERIAL WAR MUSEUM

Above: Poster: *Libération* by Phili. France, 1944.

Right: Crematorium Dachau
Concentration Camp, Germany.
PHOTOGRAPH: ARNOLD SCHWARTZMAN

Right: Survivors on their way
to Palestine, their new
homeland. 1945.
NATIONAL ARCHIVES

*Opposite: Human Laundry,
Belsen, April 1945,*
painting by Doris Zinkeisen.
Great Britain.
IMPERIAL WAR MUSEUM

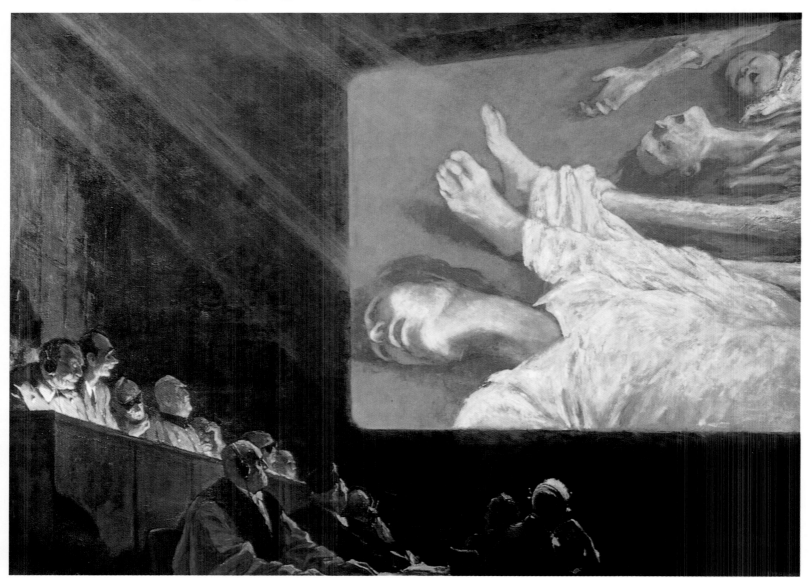

Left: The Nuremberg Trial, 1946, painted by Dame Laura Knight. Great Britain.

Opposite: The Indictment: War Criminals and Their Defenders at the Nuremberg Trials, painting by Probiry Krylov, Mikhail Kupryanov, and Nikolai Sokolov. Russia.

On October 18, 1945, the Nuremberg trials began. The defendants pleaded "Nicht schuldig" (not guilty).

There are constant reminders of
D-Day in Normandy today:

Right: One of two stained glass
memorial windows in the 12th
century Norman church of
Ste Mère Eglise.
The window commemorating
the US 82nd Airborne Division
landing on the morning of
June 6, 1944, was designed by
Paul Renaud, son of the town's
Mayor in 1944.

Far right top: Remnants of a
British "Mulberry" harbor.
Arromanches.

Far right bottom: Memorial
marker, Kilometer 00.
Utah Beach.
PHOTOGRAPH: ARNOLD SCHWARTZMAN

Above: Postcards recall the
events of June 6, 1944, outside
the "Overlord" souvenir shop.
Arromanches.
PHOTOGRAPH: ARNOLD SCHWARTZMAN

Opposite, *above*:
The "Café Bar du 6 Juin" on
rue General D. D. Eisenhower
Place du 6 Juin in Ste Mère Eglise.

Opposite, below: The "Overlord"
souvenir shop. Arromanches.
PHOTOGRAPH: ARNOLD SCHWARTZMAN

RUE
DU GÉNÉRAL
D.D. EISENHOWER
C.t OPÉRATION OVERLORD
6 JUIN 1944

PLACE
du 6 JUIN

CAFÉ BAR du 6 JUIN

SOUVENIRS   OVERLORD   LIBRAIRIE

Right: Sheet music:
We're Gonna Hang Out The Washing On The Siegfried Line.
Great Britain, 1939.
© THE PETER MAURICE MUSIC COMPANY LTD.

Below: A British soldier hanging out his washing on one of the German 88 mm gun emplacements on the beach at Courseulles-sur-Mer, Normandy. June 11, 1944.
IMPERIAL WAR MUSEUM   B5327

Remnants of German batteries along the Normandy coast:

Right top: German battery in Asnelles with floating "Mulberry" harbors in the background.

Center: Observation and gun bunker, Gold Beach.

Bottom: A derelict bunker in the sand dunes.

Opposite: One of several large German gun batteries at Longues, Normandy.

PHOTOGRAPH: ARNOLD SCHWARTZMAN

Right top: Observation and gun bunker, Gold Beach, Normandy.

Center: German gun emplacement, Battérie de Crisbecq, Normandy.
PHOTOGRAPH: ARNOLD SCHWARTZMAN

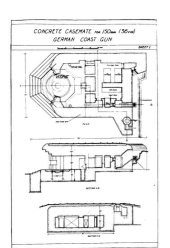

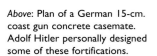

Above: Plan of a German 15-cm. coast gun concrete casemate. Adolf Hitler personally designed some of these fortifications.

Right and opposite: A collapsed gun emplacement, Battérie de Crisbecq.
PHOTOGRAPH: ARNOLD SCHWARTZMAN

Above: Shoulder patch of the U.S. 82nd Airborne Division "All American".

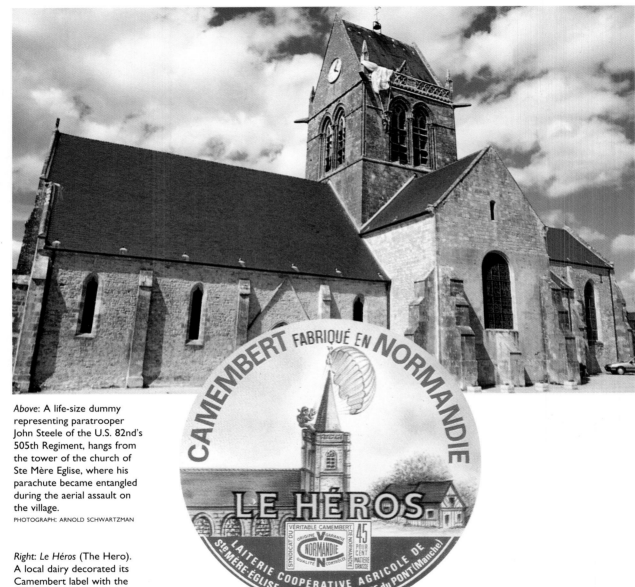

Above: Stained glass window commemorating the 25th anniversary of the D-Day invasion. Church of Ste Mère Eglise, Normandy.

PHOTOGRAPH: ARNOLD SCHWARTZMAN

Above: A life-size dummy representing paratrooper John Steele of the U.S. 82nd's 505th Regiment, hangs from the tower of the church of Ste Mère Eglise, where his parachute became entangled during the aerial assault on the village.

PHOTOGRAPH: ARNOLD SCHWARTZMAN

Right: Le Héros (The Hero). A local dairy decorated its Camembert label with the U.S. paratrooper's unfortunate landing.

Far left: British troops cross "Pegasus Bridge" over the Caen Canal. The code name for Caen Canal was "Rugger," and the Orne River was "Cricket."
IMPERIAL WAR MUSEUM   B5240

Left: "Pegasus Bridge" over the Orne Canal. 1993.
PHOTOGRAPH: ARNOLD SCHWARTZMAN

Above: Sign on the wall of the Gondrée Cafe, "Pegasus Bridge."
PHOTOGRAPH: ARNOLD SCHWARTZMAN

Left: Crashed gliders—The landing zone at Ranville, 1944, painting by Albert Richards. Great Britain.
IMPERIAL WAR MUSEUM

Right: Commemorative stamp honoring the bravery of four chaplains who went down with the U.S. transport ship Dorchester on February 3, 1943. U.S.A., 1948.

These IMMORTAL CHAPLAINS ...
INTERFAITH IN ACTION
3¢ UNITED STATES POSTAGE 3¢

Above: Insignia of a U.S. Armed Forces Jewish Chaplain.

In the early hours of the morning of February 3, 1943, a torpedo struck the U.S. transport ship Dorchester, crossing the North Atlantic with 902 troops on board.

Four Army chaplains—two Protestants, a Jew, and a Roman Catholic—after working to distribute life jackets and helping to direct the frightened men, gave up their own life belts to those without.

Surviving eyewitnesses relate how the four chaplains, Lt. George L. Fox, a Methodist; Lt Clarke V. Poling, a Dutch Reformed minister; Alexander D. Goode, a rabbi; and Lt. John P. Washington, a Roman Catholic priest; clung together with their arms linked and their heads bowed in prayer, as the ship went down.

Right: Stained glass window of a Star of David made up of military decoration ribbons, at the Headquarters of the British Association of Jewish Ex-Servicemen and Women. Designed by Abram Games. Great Britain.
PHOTOGRAPH: REG GOULD

Above: Royal Army Chaplain's Corps cap badge (Jewish). Great Britain.

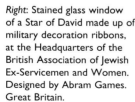

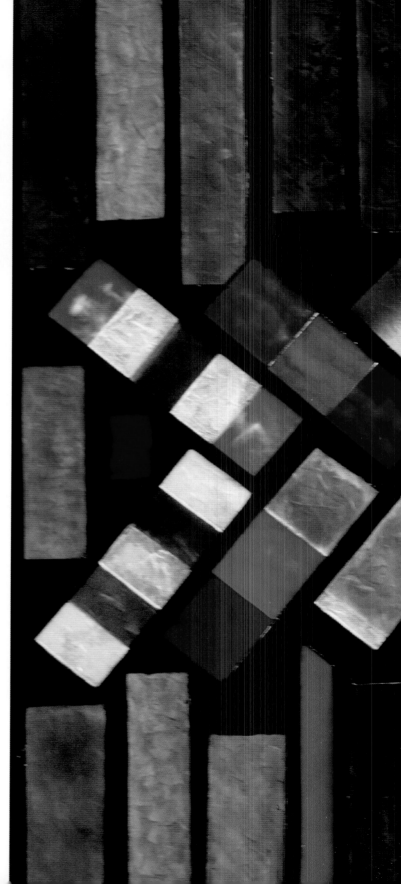

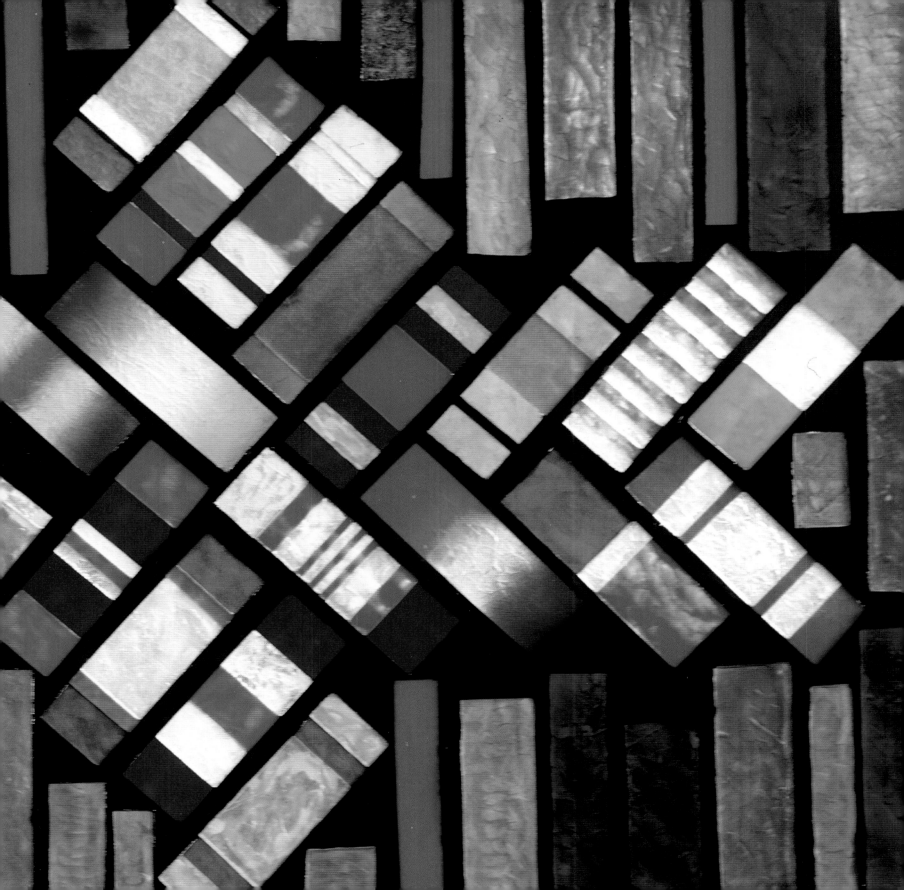

Right: Headstone of a German soldier who died on D-Day, June 6, 1944, one of a number in the Commonwealth War Graves Commission Cemetery, Bayeux.
PHOTOGRAPH: ARNOLD SCHWARTZMAN

Above: Headstone of a German Jewish soldier who fell in World War I. Rödelsee, Germany
PHOTOGRAPH: ARNOLD SCHWARTZMAN

Left, opposite bottom left, and opposite right: In the largest German cemetery in Normandy, over 21,000 dead are buried, including 296 in a mass grave under a grass mound in the center of the cemetery. La Cambe, Normandy.
PHOTOGRAPH: ARNOLD SCHWARTZMAN

Above: Commemorative postage stamp. Luxembourg.

Above: Poster:
Invasion: Cimetière des Alliés (Invasion: Allied cemetery). Germany.

Right: Headstone of an American who served with the British R.A.F. (Royal Air Force). Commonwealth War Graves Commission Cemetery. Bayeux, France.
PHOTOGRAPH: ARNOLD SCHWARTZMAN

Above: Film poster:
A Yank in the R.A.F. U.S.A., 1941.

Above: Poster: *War Bonds Are Cheaper Than Wooden Crosses.*
U.S. TREASURY

Opposite: One of a number of grave markers bearing a Star of David among the 9,386 American war dead buried in the Normandy American Cemetery in Colleville-sur-Mer. The cemetery site was chosen for its location on top of the cliff overlooking Omaha Beach.
PHOTOGRAPH: ARNOLD SCHWARTZMAN

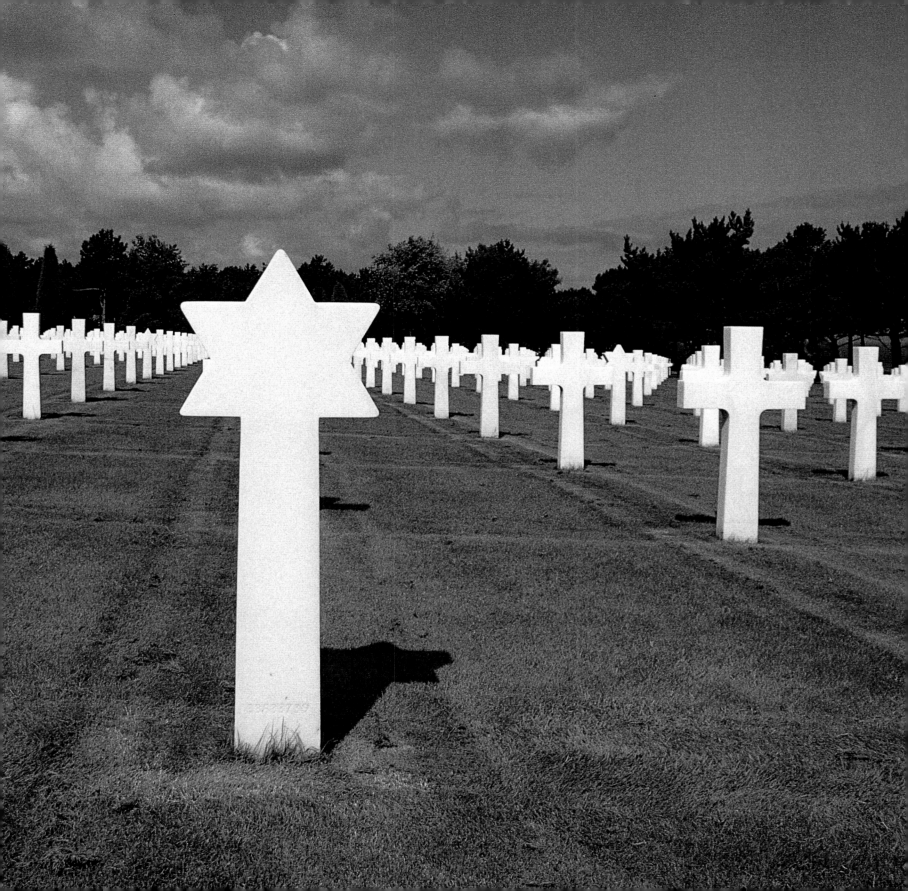

'33 January 30 – Adolf Hitler appointed Chancellor of Germany

'34 August 2 – Hitler proclaims himself Führer und Reichskanzler (Leader and Reich Chancellor)

'35 September 15 – "Nuremberg Laws": anti-Jewish racial laws enacted

'36 March 7 – Germany marches into the Rhineland
October 25 – Hitler and Mussolini form Rome-Berlin Axis

'38 March 13 – Anschluss (incorporation of Austria into the Reich)
September 30 – Munich Conference: Great Britain and France agree to German occupation of the Sudetenland
November 9-10 – Kristallnacht (Night of Broken Glass): anti-Jewish pogrom in Germany, Austria, and the Sudetenland

'39 March 15 – Germany occupies Czechoslovakia
August 23 – Molotov-Ribbentrop Pact signed: non-aggression pact between the Soviet Union and Germany
September 1 – Beginning of World War II: Germany invades Poland

'40 April 9 – Germany occupies Denmark and southern Norway
May 10 – Germany invades the Netherlands, Belgium, Luxembourg, and France
June 22 – France surrenders
August 8 – Battle of Britain begins

'41 April 6 – Germany attacks and occupies Yugoslavia and Greece
June 22 – Germany invades the Soviet Union

December 7 – Japan attacks Pearl Harbor
December 8 – United States and Great Britain declare war on Japan
December 11 – Germany and Italy declare war on United States

'42 January 20 – Wannsee Conference in Berlin: Reinhard Heydrich outlines plan to annihilate Europe's Jews—"the Final Solution"

'43 January 3 – Polish government-in-exile sends urgent message to Pope Pius XII asking him to denounce German atrocities against the Jews; Pope remains silent
January 14-23 – Roosevelt, Churchill, and the Combined Chiefs of Staff meet at Casablanca to plan future Allied strategy
February 2 – German Army surrenders at Stalingrad

Above: Stamp commemorating Hitler's birthday. Germany.

"Judenstern" (Jewish star). Germany.
SIMON WIESENTHAL CENTER

Right: Letter "J" stamped on Jewish passports. Germany.

Italian Axis leader Benito Mussolini.

Far right: Record label: *Remember Pearl Harbor.*
RCA MANUFACTURING CO. INC.

Far right: "Giftgas" label of poison gas canister from Auschwitz-Birkenau concentration camp. Poland.

ILLUSTRATION: ARNOLD SCHWARTZMAN

'44 January 9 – Winston Churchill and Charles de Gaulle meet in Marrakesh, Morocco, to discuss forthcoming invasion
January 16 – Dwight D. Eisenhower assumes command of Allied Expeditionary Forces
January 22 – Allied Forces invade coastal area around Anzio, Italy
March 19 – Germany occupies Hungary
April 13 – Allied aircraft begin series of attacks on German coast artillery units in Normandy
May 11 – Major offensive launched by Allied forces in Central Italy
May 31 – Allied troops board ships for Normandy invasion; Allied bombing prior to Normandy invasion begins
June 4 – U.S. Fifth Army enters Rome
June 6 – D-DAY: Allied invasion at Normandy— greatest amphibious operation in military history;

Beginn der Invasion
Sofortiges Einsetzen der Abwehr

Germany bombs the Florence, Italy, synagogue;

A transport with 1,800 Greek Jews, 90 percent of the Jewish population from the Island of Corfu, leaves for Auschwitz
August 25 – Paris liberated
October 25 – Britain, Russia, and U.S. re-establish formal diplomatic relations with Italy
November 1 – President Franklin D. Roosevelt elected for fourth term as president
December 17-18 – Battle of the Bulge

'45 January 20 – Roosevelt inaugurated for fourth term
January 30 – Hitler's last radio broadcast, marking the twelfth anniversary of his accession to power
March 20 – Hitler's last public appearance
April 12 – Roosevelt dies
April 25 – United Nations

Conference on International Organization opens in San Francisco
April 28 – Benito Mussolini executed by Italian partisans
April 30 – Hitler commits suicide
May 7 – German High Command surrenders unconditionally
May 8 – War in Europe declared ended; V-E Day proclaimed
May 9 – All fighting officially ends in Europe
June 26 – U.N. charter signed at San Francisco conference.
August 6 – Atomic bomb dropped on Hiroshima
August 8 – Soviet Union declares war on Japan effective August 9
August 9 – Atomic bomb dropped on Nagasaki
August 14 – Japan agrees to unconditional surrender
August 15 – V-J Day proclaimed: World War II ends

Above: "Victory,"
The Stars and Stripes.
U.S.A., May 8, 1945.
SIMON WIESENTHAL CENTER

Victory Celebrations program.
Great Britain, June 8, 1946.
JOHN FROST HISTORICAL NEWSPAPER SERVICE

Far left: Poster: "Start of the invasion. Immediate action by the defence forces."
Berlin, Germany, June 6, 1944.
IMPERIAL WAR MUSEUM

Left: "War Ends!"
Los Angeles Examiner.
U.S.A., August 15, 1945.
JIM HEIMANN

BIBLIOGRAPHY

Above: Statue of Air Vice-Marshal Arthur "Bomber" Harris, Head of British Bomber Command during World War II. The statue had been vandalized by Neo-Nazis, who daubed the word "Sionist" (sic) on the plinth.
St, Clement Danes, London, 1992.
PHOTOGRAPH: ARNOLD SCHWARTZMAN

WORLD WAR II:

Churchill, Winston S. *The Second World War.* 5 vols. Boston: Houghton-Mifflin, 1948-1953

Cohen, Stan. *V for Victory: America's Home Front During World War II.* Missoula, Montana: Pictorial Histories Publishing Company Inc., 1991

Deighton, Len. *Battle of Britain.* New York: Coward, McCann & Geoghegan, 1st U.S. ed. 1980

Deighton, Len. *Blood, Tears and Folly: An Objective Look at World War II.* New York: Harper, Collins, 1993

Eisenhower, Dwight D. *Crusade in Europe.* Garden City, N.Y.: Doubleday, 1948

Gilbert, Martin. *The Second World War: A Complete History.* New York: Henry Holt, 1989

Goralski, Robert. *World War II Almanac 1931-1945: A Political and Military Record.* New York: G.P. Putnam's Sons, 1981

Hogg, Ian, and Bryan Perrett. *Encyclopedia of the Second World War.* Novato, CA: Presidio, 1989

Keegan, John, ed. *Who Was Who in World War II.* London: Bison, 1978

WWII: Time-Life Books History of the Second World War. New York: Prentice Hall Press, 1989

Zentner, Christian and Friedemann Bedürftig, eds. *The Encyclopedia of the Third Reich.* 2 vols. New York: Macmillan, 1991

D-DAY:

Baxter, Colin F. *The Normandy Campaign, 1944: A Selected Bibliography.* New York: Greenwood Press, 1992

Badsey, Stephen. *D-Day: From the Normandy Beaches to the Liberation of France.* New York: BDD Promotional Book Company, Inc., 1993

Boussel, Patrice. *D-Day Beaches Revisited.* Garden City, N.Y.: Doubleday, 1966.

Breuer, William B. *Hoodwinking Hitler: The Normandy Deception.* Westport, Conn.: Praeger, 1993

Chandler, David G., and James Lawton Collins, Jr., eds. *The D-Day Encyclopedia.* New York: Simon & Schuster, 1994

Collier, Richard. *D-Day: June 6, 1944: The Normandy Landings.* London: Cassell, 1992.

Hastings, Max. *Overlord: D-Day and the Battle for Normandy.* New York: Simon & Schuster, 1984

Hastings, Max. *Victory in Europe: D-Day to VE-Day.* Boston: Little, Brown, 1985

Keegan, John. *Six Armies in Normandy: From D-Day to the Liberation of Paris.* New York: Viking Press, 1982

Nalty, Bernard C., ed. *D-Day: Operation Overlord: From the Landing at Normandy to the Liberation of Paris.* New York: Smithmark Publishers Inc, 1993

Ryan, Cornelius. *The Longest Day: June 6, 1944.* New York: Simon and Schuster, 1959

HOLOCAUST:

Arad, Yitzhak, ed. *The Pictorial History of the Holocaust.*
New York: Macmillan, 1990

Dawidowicz, Lucy S. *The War Against the Jews.*
New York: Bantam Books, 1986.

Edelheit, Hershel and Abraham J. Edelheit.
*A World in Turmoil: An Integrated Chronology of the
Holocaust and World War II.*
New York: Greenwood Press, 1991

Gilbert, Martin. *The Holocaust: A History of the Jews
of Europe During the Second World War.* New York:
Holt, Rinehart and Winston, 1985

Gilbert, Martin. *Atlas of the Holocaust.* 1st U.S. ed.
New York: William Morrow and Company, 1993

Grobman, Alex, and Daniel Landes.
Genocide: Critical Issues of the Holocaust. Los Angeles:
Simon Wiesenthal Center, 1983; Chappaqua, N.Y.:
Rossel Books, 1983

Gutman, Israel, ed. *Encyclopedia of the Holocaust.*
New York: Macmillan, 1991

Hilberg, Raul. *The Destruction of the European Jews.*
3 vols. New York: Holmes & Meier, 1985

Levin, Nora. *The Holocaust: The Destruction
of European Jewry, 1933-1945.* New York:
Schocken Books, 1973

Segev, Tom. *The Seventh Million: The Israelis and
the Holocaust.* New York: Hill and Wang, 1993

Left: D-Day Monument,
Omaha Beach, Normandy.
PHOTOGRAPH: ARNOLD SCHWARTZMAN

THIS BOOK IS DEDICATED TO THE MEN AND WOMEN WHO SACRIFICED THEIR LIVES FOR THE CAUSE OF FREEDOM, AND TO THE VICTIMS OF THE NAZI HOLOCAUST.

Right: Postage stamps commemorating the fiftieth anniversary of D-Day. Great Britain, 1994.
COURTESY ROYAL MAIL

ACKNOWLEDGMENTS:

Academy of Motion Picture Arts and Sciences; Apollo Verlag Paul Lincke, Berlin; BBC Publications; Bison Picture Library; Bradbury Wood Ltd.; Bill Brandt; Bundesarchiv Koblenz; Daily Express; Daily Mail; Her Majesty Queen Elizabeth II: *The Way We Were*, BBC Broadcast Radio 4, May 8, 1985; Ealing Studios; Evening News; Irwin Dash Music Co. Ltd; John Frost Historical Newspaper Collection; Imperial War Museum; Lawrence Wright Music Publishers; Library of Congress; Los Angeles Examiner; Los Angeles Times; Magnum Photos Inc.; Miller Music Corporation; Musicraft Corporation: National Archives; New Statesman; New York Post; New York Times; Peter Maurice Music Co. Ltd; Popperphoto; Public Record Office, London; Remick Music Corporation; Robert Hunt Library; Royal Mail; Santly-Joy Inc.; Simon Wiesenthal Center Archives; Stars and Stripes; Sunday Times Magazine; Tate Gallery/Art Resources; Time/Life; Tretyakov Gallery; Ullstein Bilderdienst; UPI/Movietone News; U.S. Postal Service; Walt Disney Studio; Wiener Library; M. Witmark & Sons.

THE AUTHOR WISHES TO EXPRESS HIS GRATEFUL THANKS TO THE MANY INDIVIDUALS AND ORGANIZATIONS WHO HAVE MOST GENEROUSLY ASSISTED IN THE PREPARATION OF THIS BOOK. SPECIAL THANKS ARE DUE TO THE FOLLOWING:

Association of Jewish Ex-Servicemen and Women (A.J.E.X.); Garry Brod; Philip Collins; EuroDollar Rent A Car; Andrew Frost; John Frost; Abram Games; Reg Gould; Paul Hamburg; Jim Heimann; Rabbi Marvin Hier; Marlene Hier; Adaire Klein; Cheryl Miller; Barry Robinson; Matthew Saxton; Hannah Schwartzman; Tommy Steele; Richard Trank; Henry Vizcarra; Michael Webb. Once again, last but not least, my deep gratitude to my wife, Isolde, for her enormous contribution to the editing and production of this book.